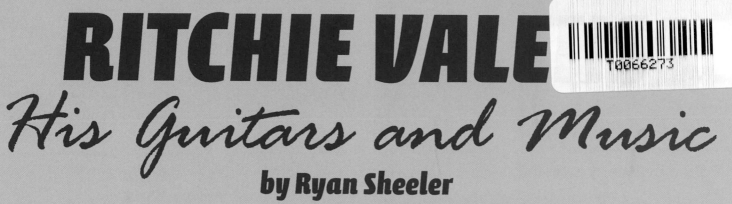

RITCHIE VALE

His Guitars and Music

by Ryan Sheeler

To access audio, visit:
www.HalLeonard.com/MyLibrary
"Enter Code"
6949-8217-2853-7142

Edited by Ronny S. Schiff

RITCHIE VALENS™
His Guitars and Music

Edited by Ronny S. Schiff

Graphic Design and Typesetting by Charylu Roberts / O.Ruby Productions

Cover Design by James Creative Group

ISBN 978-1-57424-380-2

Published by Centerstream Publishing,
P.O. Box 17878
Anaheim Hills, CA 92817
714.779-9390
www.centerstream-usa.com
centerstrm@aol.com

Distributed Worldwide by Hal Leonard LLC

EXCLUSIVELY DISTRIBUTED BY

7777 W. BLUEMOUND RD. P.O. BOX 13819 MILWAUKEE, WI 53213

Table of Contents

Introduction

I am part of the generation that came after the "Golden Age" of rock 'n' roll (1954–1959). Born and raised primarily in Central Iowa, ironically, not that far from Clear Lake and Mason City. My parents were in their junior high and high school years in late 1950s into the mid-1960s. So, when I was a young child, my first exposure to rock or pop of any kind was the music of my parents. We were very fortunate to have some great radio stations out of Des Moines that played that original "oldies" rock music, country and some R&B: 1350-AM KRNT, 1460-AM KSO, and 93.3-FM KIOA, all out of Des Moines. A lot of weekend drives were spent with the family with those stations on the dial.

I took up the guitar at age eight, because our next-door neighbor was a classical guitar teacher. I was hesitant at first, but soon warmed up to the lessons and to the guitar. Sometime later, my teacher moved away, and she recommended another teacher in town who was more of a rock player. Plus, by then I had gotten hooked on Chuck Berry, Bo Diddley, The Ventures, Eddie Cochran and Buddy Holly. As the years went on, I became more interested in the rock and blues guitarists of my generation, like Eddie Van Halen, Stevie Ray Vaughan, Steve Vai, Ted Nugent, Jimmy Page, Eric Clapton and many others. However, that early exposure to that first generation of rock guitar really stayed with me through the years.

Somewhere during those early formative years, though I can't remember exactly when, I heard "La Bamba." Like millions of other kids down through the years, that opening guitar riff was one of those that got stuck in my head. Along came the year 1987, and I was going into eighth grade that fall in the northern suburbs of Chicago. That summer, the movie *La Bamba* hit the theaters and all of my friends and I loved it. The title track and all of Ritchie's music in the movie was updated and re-done with skill and respect by Los Lobos. At all our school dances, their versions of "La Bamba," "Come on, Let's Go," and "Donna" were in regular rotation, along with all the other Top 40 tunes of the day. I had five years of guitar under my belt then, so it didn't take too long until I had those songs down well enough to perform.

I was a naturally inquisitive kid and loved reading, especially books about music, so I began to dig back and read about Ritchie Valens. Somewhere along the way, it came to me, probably by way of my parents and also by reading, that Ritchie was one of the people killed in the same plane crash of 1959 that killed Buddy Holly…a crash that occurred in Clear Lake, Iowa, not 70 miles north of where I grew up in Ames.

As the years went by, I moved back to Iowa, played in bands, went to college, and moved on with life, but that summer of 1987 still stuck with me. As an undergraduate and graduate, I studied music at Iowa State and especially enjoyed the History of Rock 'n' Roll class taught by my major professor, Dr. David Stuart. I assisted him in the class, and later took it over myself. I have always had a deep interest in music history and, in particular, pop and rock music history.

Through all my playing days and continuing research, I really grew to love and appreciate the music of Ritchie Valens. Ritchie had a youthful energy and big sound to his music, and he was always photographed with a guitar, usually it was a Sunburst Fender Stratocaster—and I loved Fenders! Buddy Holly was the first "rocker" to adopt the Stratocaster or "Strat," I figured Ritchie couldn't be too far behind. Over the subsequent decade, through interviews, films, and books, I heard and read a lot of anecdotal evidence that Ritchie was a great guitarist, even for being young and untrained. However, I found the research on Ritchie and his music to be minuscule and hard to find, to say nothing of information on his guitar playing itself. So, I began to think of questions like:

- How did Ritchie take up the guitar?
- Who were some of his favorite guitarists?
- What guitars did he own and how did he come by them?
- How much of his own guitar work did he perform on his records?
- What did other people with whom he toured or played think of his playing?
- Who has his guitars now?
- Why should he be remembered as a guitarist?

I never really knew how much of Ritchie's music featured his own guitar work. I knew that at least some of it was done by the famous Los Angeles session players René Hall and Carol Kaye. But the release of *Ritchie Valens in Concert at Pacoima Jr. High* originally in 1960—a hidden gem of a rough live album—did much to reveal to the world how good a guitarist Ritchie was, even at 17 years old.

Therefore, I figured that this aspect of Ritchie's music has never been covered in depth, and that the topic of Ritchie's guitars and guitar playing might make an interesting and important contribution to the research. I do believe that Ritchie Valens was a very important part of the first five years of the formation of rock 'n' roll and that he should stand right along with Chuck Berry, Bo Diddley, Buddy Holly, Carl Perkins, Eddie Cochran, Scotty Moore, and Cliff Gallup as the best and most important electric guitar players of the original rock 'n' roll era. This is what I hope to contribute with this book. a tremendous labor of love for me. As I studied, listened, took notes, wrote letters, made phone calls, transcribed interviews, listened to Ritchie's songs repeatedly, I realized all over again how much I enjoy his music.

In March 2019, "La Bamba" was named to the National Recording Registry of the Library of Congress as part of a group of recordings "…worthy of preservation because of their cultural, historic and aesthetic importance to the nation's recorded sound heritage." This great honor further solidifies Ritchie's legacy and his pivotal contribution made by combining his heritage sound with early rock 'n' roll; thus, paving the way for generations that followed.

Thanks for joining me on this unique journey down a road through music history.

CHAPTER 1
Ritchie Valens — His Story

There are a few fine biographies of Ritchie Valens in various books (the best is Beverly Mendheim's excellent *Ritchie Valens: The First Latino Rocker*—hers was the first full-length biography about Ritchie). I have corresponded at-length with Beverly about Ritchie and his guitars for this project, and she has been very gracious in helping me with this project. As any musician, historian, or musicologist will tell you, music (or any art for that matter) does not exist in a vacuum. It is best to not separate the study of art from the culture in which it was created. Music is not only the product of God-given talent, nurturing and hard work, but it is also a product of the environment and of the times.

Richard Steven Valenzuela was born May 13, 1941 at Los Angeles County Osteopathic Hospital, north of downtown Los Angeles, to Joseph Steven ("Steve") and Concepcion Reyes Valenzuela. His father worked as a miner, ranch hand/cowboy, and tree surgeon, and had a mining accident, which left him hurt severely. Ritchie's parents separated when he around three years old, and he lived with his father in Pacoima. His father encouraged young Richie's (without the "t") burgeoning musical talents by having him take up the guitar and singing. Young Richie was very shy, but his father was stern-but-loving in encouragement. Richie's father was sick much of the time with diabetes and several other ailments and passed away in 1951.

What happened next, after Ritchie's father's death, is slightly difficult to track and varies from source-to-source. It is held commonly that Ritchie's mother moved into Steve's house in Pacoima with her older son (from a previous marriage) Bob Morales, and Ritchie's younger sisters, Connie and Irma. There is some confusion as to the general timing of these events—some accounts having Ritchie staying with other relatives until he was approximately 11 years old or so. He spent a lot of time with his aunt and uncle, Ernestine and Lelo Reyes—his relationship with them would continue well into his famous years and would be proven to be a pivotal influence in Ritchie's life.

A rather fortuitous by-product of living with his relatives and extended family is that this environment helped encourage Ritchie's innate talent for music. He was encouraged in his music by relatives on his mother's and father's sides of the family. There is varying information on how Ritchie got started with the guitar. He had an early cigar-box guitar that may have been made by one of his relatives. His cousin Dickie Cota taught him guitar chords and some traditional Mexican songs including "La Bamba." An uncle, John Lozano, is mentioned as giving Ritchie some guidance on the guitar as well. And his aunt Ernestine mentioned another relative giving Ritchie a guitar. As he began to grow in his love for guitars, he would practice long hours and sing and play to his younger sisters. He developed a love for the guitar very quickly and played it every chance he got.

Pacoima Junior High School (now Pacoima Middle School) opened its doors in 1954 and Richie entered as a 7th grader. By this time, Ritchie had started to carry his guitar—an off-white Harmony acoustic—to class, where he would play and sing between classes and for various informal gatherings. He had taken a liking to woodshop class and had also bought a cheap Harmony H44 Stratotone (more in the "Ritchie's Guitars" chapter). No pictures exist of this guitar with its original paint finish, but it is well-known that Ritchie refinished this guitar to a dark green in woodshop class. And somewhere along the way, he picked up a second-hand guitar amp ("ampli-fier"—unknown model likely some type of Sears or Montgomery Ward model or small Fender Champ). He also began to develop a taste for rock 'n' roll and R&B of that early period: early Little Richard, Chuck Berry and Bo Diddley, and the other R&B and early rock performers includ-ing doo-wop groups such as the Penguins, Orioles, Robins (later Coasters) and lesser known groups such as the Medallions and Robert and Johnny ("We Belong Together," which Ritchie would later cover himself).

> *Of historical note: In January 1957, there was a mid-air plane collision that occurred in Pacoima approximately over the grounds of Pacoima Junior High School. A Douglas DC-7B collided with a USAF Northrop F-89 Scorpion in mid-air over the San Fernando Valley. Wreckage from the Douglas DC-7B rained down on the school playground of Pacoima Junior High School—the crew and several schoolchildren were killed and scores more injured. Ritchie was not in school on that day, he was away attending a family funeral for his maternal grandfather, Frank Reyes. By most accounts, this incident, along with seeing planes flying too close to the roads in the Valley, had frightened Ritchie.*

Ritchie entered San Fernando High School as a sophomore in the fall of 1957 (in those days, high schools were often only three grades instead of the four common today). That fall, he joined-up with a group of musicians that called themselves the Silhouettes. It has been said that Ritchie started the group, but this is commonly held as false, since the group was active in the neighborhood before Ritchie joined. Gil Rocha was the leader of the group, although historical accounts vary between his accounts and that of Bill Jones, another member. The Silhouettes with Gil and Ritchie and a slightly-variable core group played dances in the San Fernando Valley from the fall of 1957 to May of 1958. They played all over the area: at the San Fernando Ameri-can Legion, San Fernando High School, Pacoima Recreation Park and elsewhere.

Completely self-taught, but with an obvious natural talent and aptitude for music, Ritchie was making a name for himself playing guitar at school functions and most anywhere they would let him play. He had been dubbed "Little Richard of the Valley," because of his love for Little Richard or "Richie and his Crying Guitar" because of his love of bending the guitar strings. Gil wanted him to bring some blues to the band, so Ritchie brought in an early version of "Big Baby Blues," and soon gained his "...Crying Guitar" nickname because of his love of the string-bend-ing blues guitar technique.

His mother was struggling financially to support Ritchie and Bob (though Bob eventu-ally moved out), along with the younger sisters Connie and Irma and newborn brother Mario. Ritchie's mother had a pension from Steve's death, and supplemented her income as a waitress. In order to raise more money to help the family, in May 1958, Ritchie and his mom decided to throw a dance party at the Pacoima Legion Hall that would feature Ritchie and the band. Gil Rocha taped the show gave the tape to a friend, Doug Macchia who also worked for Bob Keane (or Keene, original name Bob Kuhn), helping him with his printing needs and business cards. Keane owned a small independent record label, Del-Fi Records, out of Los Angeles. Just a short time later in a matter of weeks, Keane was able to see that Ritchie was playing a local amateur talent show and gathering at the old Rennie's Theater in San Fernando (later to-be-renamed the Crest Theater and then El Azteca). Ritchie stood up on the theater stage before the matinee on a Saturday morning, playing his guitar through a small second-hand little amp (most likely a

Fender Champ™—see Chapter 2) and entertained a gathering of his friends and classmates. Ritchie had won two of these "shows" in a row, and the third time Bob Keane came to see Ritchie. Keane sat in the back, and was very impressed by the energetic young boy and thought about getting him to record. Keane spoke with (shy) Ritchie briefly, and gave him a business card, and thought nothing more of it. Thankfully, Ritchie followed up on the meeting and went out to Keane's home studio, bringing some his friends in The Silhouettes with him.

Keane had a small studio in his home, but in that small space he had an Ampex 601-2 reel-to-reel, 2-track stereo recorder and two Telefunken microphones—a very nice small studio setup in those days. Ritchie brought his Harmony H44 Stratotone and little amp to the session. Since Richie was completely self-taught and came from musical traditions that were orally shared and passed-down vs. written down, he didn't have any complete songs for Keane, just some riffs on the guitar and some very loose parts of verses and bits of lyrics (again, supposedly, none of these written down either)

Ritchie with his raw talent, had rapidly absorbed the sounds of Elvis, Chuck Berry, his favorite Little Richard, Bo Diddley and other greats of the day. He had developed an energetic guitar sound with a unique style all his own. Keane set out to help the young musician on songwriting ideas with the intent on turning Ritchie's ideas into full-fledged songs. For several weeks after their initial setting, Bob (now called "Bobbo") and Ritchie met regularly for songwriting sessions, and they developed a trust and bond as mentor and mentee. Keane even visited the Valenzuela household and was able to meet Ritchie's family, it was important for them to see that Ritchie was being taken care of and nurtured in his gifts and talents.

Out of these sessions emerged the initial seeds for "Come on, Let's Go." The title and main hook came from a saying that Ritchie and his family used a lot around their home. Keane immediately knew the idea could be a smash hit; even in its rawest form he could see the potential. It is often mentioned that there was no structure only the initial line and hook "Come on, Let's Go"—and so Bob got Ritchie to work through it and together they eventually came up with words and a melody. (Note: But it is worth mentioning here that the first demo of "Come on, Let's Go" shows up on the *Ritchie Valens: The Last Tapes* release that Del-Fi released years later; it is the first audition demo that Ritchie recorded of the song and is also the same version spliced together with live crowd noise on the *Ritchie Valens: In Concert at Pacoima Jr. High* album. This original demo version actually shows that the song was fairly well developed, guitar riffs and all, when Ritchie brought it in.)

In late May 1958, Bob Keane signed Ritchie to a contract with his label Del-Fi. It was then that Keane made the decision to shorten "Valenzuela" to "Valens" and to add the "t" to Ritchie. This was done to make Ritchie's name appear less ethnic, because Keane knew that DJs would not play his records if they knew he was Latino, after seeing his name. And soon they went into Gold Star Studios (home to Phil Spector's Wall of Sound and many famous sessions just a few years later in the 1960s). For these sessions, Keane assembled a top-notch group around Ritchie: Drummer Earl Palmer, guitarist/arranger René Hall, guitarists Carol Kaye, Irving Ashby, bassists Buddy Clark, Red Callender, and pianist Ernie Freeman. This group was very well-versed in jazz; all of them were working strong jazz musicians on the California scene. This core group of musicians would form the backup group for all of

Ritchie's Del-Fi sessions. Earl Palmer and René Hall were already respected New Orleans jazz players who had come to California in search of more and better gigs. Earl Palmer and Carol Kaye, in particular, went on become part of a group of Los Angeles session musicians, the Wrecking Crew, who played on hundreds of rock, pop, and movie sessions in Los Angeles over the next 10–15 years.

René Hall would prove to be a pivotal addition with his arranging ability and talent on both guitar and bass. Hall had several hits using the new Danelectro Longhorn 6-string bass—a guitar-type instrument made out of a material called Masonite. The Longhorn 6-string bass model had strings tuned an octave lower than a standard guitar. The sound was an interesting hybrid of a bass and regular electric guitar sound; a sound that blended very well with Clark's upright bass work. The "Dano" sound added extra heft and drive to Ritchie's riffs and when combined with Palmer's drumming and Kaye's and Clark's rhythm, a new sound was born. You can hear Hall's Danelectro double Ritchie's riffs on many of his songs, especially on "Come on, Let's Go," "La Bamba," and Ritchie's version of "Bony Moronie," among others.

According to Keane, "Come on, Let's Go" took several dozen edits or so to get right (editing tape meant splicing it with a razor blade in those days!)—only because Ritchie never did it the same way, let alone twice in the studio. Ritchie and Bob chose "Framed" for the B-Side (1954, written by Leiber and Stoller, originally sung by The Robins, who spun off into The Coasters). After editing the disc, Bob took a reference disc to KFWB in Los Angeles where DJs Gene Weed and Ted Quillin really liked the disc and began to give it substantial airplay. The song quickly became a massive hit in the Los Angeles area—due, in no small part, to the Latino population in the area. The song soon went nationwide and was a "Pick of the Week" in *Billboard* in September 1958, climbing into the higher levels of the charts in a matter of weeks.

Because his music career was taking off so quickly, in the fall of 1958 Ritchie was soon finding that he did not have time for school. So, he had to leave Pacoima High. He was soon playing some very good gigs at larger venues such as Pacific Ocean Park (Santa Monica) and El Monte Legion Stadium. In October, Keane and Ritchie went on a concert tour of the East Coast, where, despite his reticence, Ritchie had to travel by air on some of the dates. On October 6th, he would appear for the first of two times on Dick Clark's "American Bandstand"; on that performance, he sang "Come on, Let's Go."

For his next hit, Valens would release a song written about his girlfriend back in Pacoima. Ritchie first met Donna Ludwig at an Igniters party. The Igniters were a "car club"—groups of kids were into cars and often street racing. Donna and Ritchie were from different neighborhoods, literally and figuratively, and had to see each other somewhat secretly, because Donna's father forbade them to officially date—Hispanic and non-Hispanics didn't date in those days. So, Ritchie had begun to write a song for his girl Donna with the beginning lines "I had a girl and Donna was her name…" He pitched his song idea to Bob Keane, and in an afternoon session, Ritchie, Bob and Herb Montei fleshed out the song (Herb was Keane's publishing partner—Kemo Music). Keane recorded a vocal and guitar demo with Ritchie at his home studio, and took it into Gold Star for overdubs a week later. With the addition of musicians Palmer, Hall, Kaye, and the others, with some nice lead fills by Ritchie, "Donna" was destined to be a smash hit. But it needed a B-side. And so, Keane and Valens came up with the idea and arrangement for "La Bamba"; the decision to include it would prove to be very fortuitous. (See Chapter 3 for more on "La Bamba.")

By October of 1958, "Donna" was starting to make a big impact on the charts thanks to another jump-start from Chuck Blore, Weed, and Quinlin at KFWB. Keane and Valens embarked another tour that took them through Chicago and other cities on a 10-city tour. During this span, "Donna" would invariably be the #1 chart topper and request in every city they passed through. By late November, the single would be back-ordered by about 100,000 copies at Del-Fi. And then the DJs started flipping the single over again, and "La Bamba" started to take off. Ritchie Valens had himself a true double-sided smash hit.

In late November 1958 through early December, Keane and Valens finished recording tracks for Ritchie's first full-length album, which would be released in 1959 as *Ritchie Valens*. In addition to the hits, "Come on, Let's Go," "Donna" and "La Bamba," there were other great songs like "Ooh, My Head," "In a Turkish Town," "Bluebirds Over the Mountain," and "Hi-Tone." After Ritchie's death, the leftover tracks from these sessions were augmented by tracks from Keane's home studio for the *Ritchie* album.

Ritchie took a brief vacation to Hawai'i, where he played the "Show of Stars" with Buddy Holly, Paul Anka and others. Returning home to California on December 10th, 1958, Ritchie played gigs at San Fernando High and Pacoima Junior High. The Pacoima Junior High show featured Ritchie on guitar and vocals with Don Phillips on drums. Ritchie's friend Gail Smith emceed the assembly—she would go on to lead Ritchie's fan club. In a rather fortuitous turn of events, the school principal recorded the Pacoima gig, which was later compiled by Keane and released as *Ritchie Valens: Live at Pacoima Junior High* in December of 1960. For Ritchie fans, this recording is truly a cherished favorite of Ritchie's recorded output. Here in a completely live and unpolished setting, the raw talent of Ritchie shows through without any aid of studio technology. It is an authentic and entertaining musical document to which to listen, and Ritchie's guitar riffs are on full display. The album is more difficult to find these days. (The more recent *Ritchie Valens: The Lost Tapes* is also a treasure trove of great Ritchie moments.)

Near the end of December 1958, Ritchie embarked on another East Coast tour. Somewhere during this time, he had picked up his sunburst Fender Stratocaster and his famous blue satin shirt stage outfit. During this stretch, he performed the famous Alan Freed "Christmas Jubilee Show" series in New York with Eddie Cochran, Jackie Wilson and a host of other rock greats. This gig was remembered for the 1987 *La Bamba* film. And, on this run, Ritchie made his second appearance on "American Bandstand" singing "Donna." "Donna"/"La Bamba" was making a major climb on the national charts by now.

In early January 1959, Ritchie recorded a few more sessions with Keane. He also appeared on NBC's "The Music Shop" and filmed a cameo appearance in Alan Freed's film *Go Johnny Go*. In his scene in the film, Ritchie is introduced to Freed by Chuck Berry. Ritchie then grabs a Gretsch guitar and sings "Ooh, My Head" to a group of girls sitting at a table.

After the filming wrapped for *Go Johnny Go*, Keane signed Ritchie up with General Artists Corporation (GAC). GAC then booked Ritchie to be a part of the upcoming "Winter Dance

Party," a tour headlined by Buddy Holly and a new group of Crickets, with Waylon Jennings, Tommy Allsup and Carl Bunch in place of Niki Sullivan, Joe B. Mauldin, and Jerry Allison. Holly was working mostly out of New York at the time and somewhat estranged from the Crickets and his manager Norman Petty, who he felt was holding his earnings. Also, on the tour were J.P. Richardson—"The Big Bopper," Dion and the Belmonts, and Frankie Sardo.

Ritchie did some more sessions on January 21st, 1959 and had a going-away party at his mother's house. After years of living in impoverished conditions, with some money advanced by Keane, Ritchie was able earlier to buy his mother a new house. Then, Ritchie flew out to Chicago to join the Winter Dance Party.

Much has been written about the Winter Dance Party tour of 1959, here's a brief summary: The tour itinerary was a major piece of poor planning. The gigs were scheduled in the ballroom circuit of the Upper Midwest with venues in Wisconsin, Minnesota, Iowa, and North Dakota among the locations. The tour planners picked some of the very worst routes between the cities. The performers travelled by converted school buses. To cap it off, the tour occurred during the very harsh winter of early 1959. The heater on the bus broke down often, as did the bus itself, causing the performers to be stranded in the cold. Often, they pulled into the venues very late with only hours to spare before they had to perform; the teenage crowd would sometimes arrive at the venues *before* the performers would arrive on their crippled bus.

A couple of weeks into the tour, conditions were unbearable. The performers were sleep-deprived, cold and unable to get their clothes washed in a timely fashion. They pulled into the Surf Ballroom in Clear Lake, Iowa on the evening of February 2nd, 1959, barely ahead of the concert start time. Sometime throughout the evening, Buddy had learned of Dwyer Flying Service out of Mason City and chartered a plane for himself, Waylon and Tommy (drummer Carl Bunch was laid up in hospital in Green Bay, Wisconsin where he'd gotten frostbitten feet). The Big Bopper, tired and sick with a cold or flu, talked Waylon Jennings out of his seat on the flight. Ritchie also wanted to fly, and asked Tommy Allsup to trade his seat several times in the evening. Allsup eventually relented, flipped a coin and lost his seat to Valens. A bit after midnight, the three performers and venue manager Carroll Anderson left the Surf for the Mason City, Iowa airport, a short distance away. There, owner Jerry Dwyer and pilot Roger Peterson, readied the Beechcraft Bonanza aircraft. The plane took off after midnight in the early morning of February 3rd, bound for the next stop of the tour at Fargo, North Dakota/Moorhead, Minnesota. The plane never made it to the destination. It crashed approximately five miles north of Clear Lake in an open field; killing Holly, Valens, Richardson, and pilot Roger Peterson. It was the first great tragedy of the rock 'n' roll era.

Ritchie's family and Bob Keane were devastated by Ritchie's death. Eventually, his songs dropped off the charts. However, the *Ritchie Valens* album was released on Del-Fi in March 1959; *Ritchie* was released in October 1959, and *Ritchie Valens: Live at Pacoima Junior High* was released later in December 1960. At the time of his death, Ritchie Valens was only 17 years old and his career lasted a total of eight months. He was buried at San Fernando Mission Cemetery, in San Fernando, California.

In 1987, director Luis Valdez along with producer Taylor Hackford, released the film *La Bamba* with Lou Diamond Phillips in the title role, Esai Morales as Bob, Danielle von Zerneck as Donna, and Rosanna DeSoto as Connie (Concepcion) Valenzuela, Ritchie's mother. Several of Ritchie's family members appear in cameos in the film. The band Los Lobos from East Los Angeles faithfully covered all of Ritchie's songs for the soundtrack, and their version of "La Bamba" hit #1 on the *Billboard Hot 100* chart in 1987. In addition, Bob Keane maintained Ritchie's image and catalog with some reissues and new compilations. Of course, Ritchie's original catalog and reissues all had a resurgence in the years after the film.

Thanks in large part due to the efforts of Ritchie's surviving family, Bob Keane, and close friends, and the continued success of the 1987 film, the music, influence and legacy of Ritchie Valens remain strong today.

Pacoima (late 1950s: View looking northeast showing the intersection of Van Nuys Boulevard and San Fernando Road).

CHAPTER 2
Ritchie's Guitars – Their History and Sound

"Ritchie's talent and ability as a guitarist were among the greatest of his time."
—Bob Keane, Del-Fi Records (liner notes of *Ritchie* album, Del-Fi Records, 1959)

Part I: Ritchie's Guitars

In the limited number of books and films available about Ritchie Valens, many people who encountered Ritchie, along with members of his family and close circle of friends, all praise Ritchie's abilities as a guitar player and his love for the instrument. And yet among all the acknowledged guitar greats of early rock, such as Chuck Berry, Bo Diddley, Carl Perkins, Scotty Moore, Buddy Holly, Eddie Cochran, Cliff Gallup and Buddy Holly, Ritchie's name is rarely mentioned. However, he left behind enough recorded work and anecdotal praise from peers to merit consideration among that group of early rock guitar legends.

Once Ritchie picked up some early skills with the guitar, thanks to some informal lessons with some members of his family, he took to the instrument quickly. Picking up on his heroes like Bo Diddley, Chuck Berry, and Eddie Cochran, and combining with the familial Mexican influences, as well as the early Southern California sounds of Dick Dale—several years before the surf sound was named as such, Ritchie fashioned a unique style all his own.

*Figure 2-1: Ritchie's most famous guitars: 1958 Gibson ES225TD and
1958/59 Fender Stratocaster (© Beverly Mendheim collection, used by permission)*

1. Epiphone Ritz Acoustic Guitar (circa 1944)

Information on this guitar was difficult to track down. The early pictures of Ritchie, like this one at a 1958 Halloween party, show an Epiphone Ritz, white archtop acoustic—a medium-to-budget-level acoustic guitar. Ritchie rented it from Cassell's Music in San Fernando, sometime in mid-1958. (Cassell's Music is still around today—see section further down). Normally finished in a natural clear finish, they were finished in opaque or off-white during the years of World War II, supposedly to hide the variance in wood quality. The Ivory/Blonde finish was only used for a limited time around 1944 *(Joe Vinikow/Archtop.com).* In the 1987 film, *La Bamba*, Lou Diamond Phillips is playing a white Harmony acoustic—a replica of this Epiphone guitar that Pat Woertink built.

Figure 2-2 Ritchie with (circa) 1944 Epiphone Ritz acoustic; Halloween Party 1958 (image © Gail Smith, used by permission)

Figure 2-3 1944 Epiphone Ritz Acoustic Guitar (Photo courtesy © Joe Vinikow, archtopcom, used by permission)

Epiphone Ritz Guitar Specifications

- Manufactured only from 1940–1944

- Finish: Original blonde finish / nitrocellulose lacquer

- Body: Solid carved Adirondack spruce top; highly-flamed, arched maple back

- Neck/Fingerboard: Solid one-piece cherry neck; Brazilian rosewood fingerboard; pearl script peghead inlay; tortoise shell body binding; solid bone nut

- Hardware: 100% original nickel hardware, includes open back tuners with ivoroid keys; trapeze tailpiece; adjustable Brazilian rosewood bridge; swirl tortoise pickguard; hex-key adjustable truss rod

Figure 2-4: The replica version of the Epiphone guitar made by Pat Woertink for Harmony Guitars and used in the 1987 film La Bamba
(image. © Jose Padilla, used by permission)

2. Harmony H44 Stratotone Electric Guitar (circa 1955)

Before he bought or received better guitars, this was Ritchie's main workhorse guitar in his early Silhouettes days and beyond. He used it on many of his early sessions with Del-Fi. It is an original Harmony H44 "Stratotone" that Ritchie purchased around 1955. Ritchie's mother bought it for him from Sears; there was a Sears store in San Fernando during the 1950s that carried them. (*Gil Rocha correspondence*, 2018-2019). The H44 was also one of the guitars that Ritchie carried around with him in school, most often in those years just before he became famous. When Gil Rocha (whose band The Silhouettes, Ritchie was a member of) first met Ritchie in 1957, Ritchie had been playing guitar for a few years already and had that guitar. There are some very brief or miniscule accounts that have Ritchie possibly getting this guitar from a pawn shop, and there were several in the area during this time, [*Founded in 1954, Traders Loan & Jewelry, 18505 Sherman Way Reseda, 1955, Bennett Pawnshop in Panorama City*]. I contacted Trader's Loan and Jewelry—who also bought out Bennett's—and they have no record of this guitar or its sale thereof dating back to the mid 1950s. *(Diane Taylor correspondence, 2019)*

It was originally gold in finish. Ritchie painted it red, but discovered he didn't like it that color. He then repainted it in wood shop class as the classic forest green guitar that we see in his promo pictures. *(Gil Rocha correspondence 2016–2017; Pat Woertink correspondence 2019)*. The original H44 was recovered by Pat Woertink, who cleaned and refinished it. Pat also built the prototype of the custom H44 Ritchie Valens reissue guitar for Harmony in the 2000s. The original guitar resides at the Grammy Museum in Los Angeles. *(Pat Woertink correspondence, 2016)*.

Specs for the Harmony H44 Stratotone (1952–1957)

From *The Harmony Database* (http://harmony.demont.net/—François Demont, used by permission)

- Dimensions:
    - Length overall: 36"
    - Width: 10 5/8"
    - Scale length: 25 1/4"
- One piece of wood "neck-through" body, with "ears" attached
- Original gold finish; refinished Chrysler green by Ritchie
- One (1) volume control; one (1) tone control
- One (1) single-coil pickup
- Special "slider" switch; treble/bass emphasis
- Rosewood fingerboard
- Rosewood bridge with compensating tailpiece

Figure 2-5: Author Beverly Mendheim with Harmony H44 Ritchie Valens signature series replica/resissue; 1992 or 1994. (© Beverly Mendheim collection, used by permission)

Figure 2-6: Richie (center; with Walter Takaki on sax, and Walter Prendez, Jr., vocals); February 1957—Ritchie with his Harmony H44 guitar and an early 1950s Fender TV Front Pro (photo courtesy of Gil Rocha, used by permission)

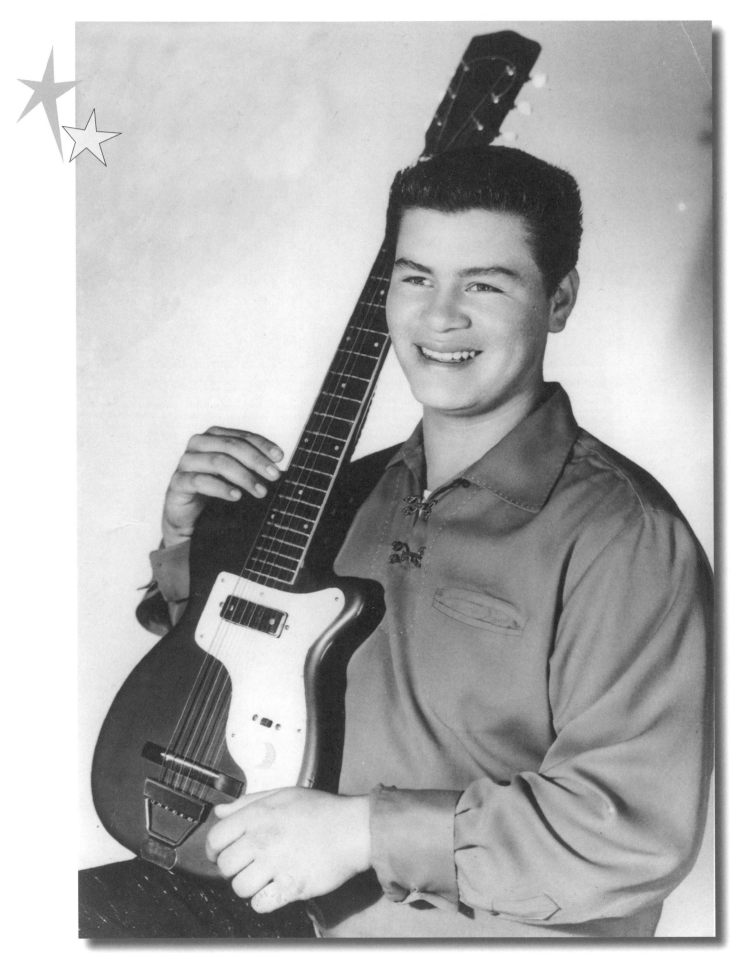

Figure 2-7: Earliest promo picture of Ritchie with Harmony H44 Stratotone guitar
(©Hi-Tone Five Corp. / C3 Entertainment, used by permission)

3. Gibson ES-175 (circa 1957–1958)

Very few pictures exist of Ritchie playing this guitar, and it was not a main guitar he used for pictures, live performance or recording. This is another guitar that Ritchie rented or borrowed from Cassell's from time to time. The Gibson ES-175 debuted in 1949 and is still in production to this day. Ritchie was using one off and on in 1958 (see image below). The well-known bassist, Carol Kaye also remembers Ritchie recording in the studio with some model of Gibson guitar that could very well have been this same ES-175. She mentioned that particular Gibson and she also remembers him with a thicker model, and the ES-225TD (see #4 below) is a much thinner guitar.

Figure 2-8: Ritchie with Gibson ES-175 electric guitar;
American Legion Hall gig in Pacoima—February 1958.
(photo courtesy of Gil Rocha, used by permission)

4. 1958 Gibson ES-225TD

The Gibson ES-225 was one of two of Ritchie's main guitars, once he became famous (the other being the Fender Stratocaster as discussed below). This is a two-pickup, middle-of-the-line, semi-hollow electric guitar made by Gibson from 1955–1959. (ES = "Electric Spanish," T = Thinline, D = Dual pickups). It was the first thin-line, hollow body electric guitar that Gibson made.

Ritchie's mother bought this for him on credit from Cassell's Music in San Fernando in October 1958. This is also the guitar Ritchie played for the *Live at Pacoima Junior High* album and is featured in several of his promotional pictures.

Figure 2-9: October 1958, receipt for Gibson ES-225 Guitar from Cassell's Music, San Fernando, CA (courtesy of Ed Intagliata, Cassell's Music, used by permission)

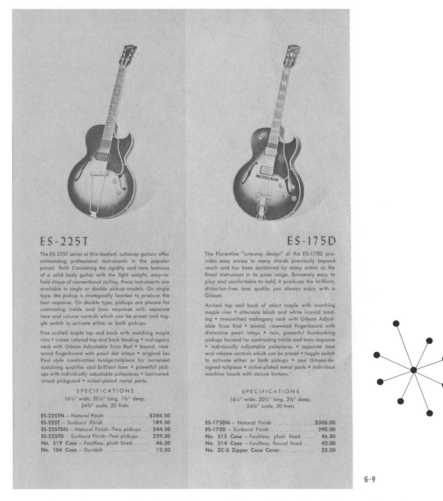

Figure 2-10: Specifications for 1958 Gibson ES-225TD—1958 Gibson Catalog (© Gibson Brands, Inc., used by permission)

Image 2-11: Ritchie and Don Phillips backstage at Pacoima Junior High
(the Live at Pacoima Junior High album); December 1958. Ritchie with his Gibson ES-225TD
(© Gail Smith collection, used by permission Hi-Tone Five Corp. / C3 Entertainment)

Figure 2-12: Ritchie with his Gibson ES-225TD, along with Bob Keane
(© Hi-Tone Five Corp. / C3 Entertainment)

5. Fender Stratocaster—1958/1959 Model

The Fender Stratocaster first appeared in 1954 and has gone on to be Fender's *crown jewel* model used by thousands of rockers and would-be rockers in the decades since its inception. Buddy Holly is commonly acknowledged as the first rock 'n' roll star to play a "Strat" guitar, and Ritchie was right behind. The Stratocaster, like its predecessor the Telecaster, was originally more popular in country and western swing bands. In the early period of rock 1954-1959, a Fender Strat guitar was a brand-new item on the market and very desirable. The guitar was a quantum leap ahead for electric guitars in look and performance. It had a customized dual-cutaway body (from the earlier Fender Precision Bass Guitar) that resembled a cross between a sports car and a spaceship in the minds of people of the time. It had three electronic pickups, with a switch to shift between combinations of them for different tones—a highly unique and innovative feature. These pickups were built around a single magnetic coil and produced a somewhat thinner sound than the P90 single-coil pickup in Ritchie's Gibson ES-225, for instance.

Ritchie Valens is famously pictured frequently with a Fender Strat, and he used the guitar often, late in his career. His groundbreaking instrumental, "Fast Freight" was recorded with the Strat guitar *(Pat Woertink correspondence 2016–2017)*. Leo Fender gave everyone (Ritchie, Buddy Holly, The Big Bopper, Dion, and many more) new Fender Strat guitars for the Winter Dance Party tour. The Winter Dance Party was booked well in advance of January 1959, and so Ritchie is pictured often with a Fender as early as very late 1958. Fender, just like rock 'n' roll itself, was not the international entity that it is today. Leo Fender had plenty of friends, acquaintances, and business contacts in the Southern California music scene—he knew who was playing his instruments and amplifiers. Dick Dale and Leo Fender worked together a lot; and Dick Dale eventually worked with and mentored Ritchie. Dale was one of the earliest Strat guitar enthusiasts on the West Coast scene and an innovator of the soon-to-come surf music craze.

All of Ritchie's promotional pictures that feature him holding the sunburst Strat guitar, date from this period, as well as a few live shots from "American Bandstand." Ritchie's two studio albums have him with the Fender Strat guitar. There are a few home movies from this timeframe with Ritchie playing that guitar. And, there are also numerous photos of Ritchie playing the Fender on various stops of The Winter Dance Party. As with the Gibson, the Fender was stolen from the Valens family several decades ago and, to date, has not been recovered.

Fender has made an American Vintage '59 Stratocaster that they've painstakingly reverse-engineered to period specs, and these would be very much like the ones Ritchie and Buddy played.

Model Name: American Vintage '59 Stratocaster® (Early '59)

- Model Number: 0111602800
- Series: Pure Vintage Series
- Colors: (0111602800) Faded 3-Color Sunburst, (Fender® Flash Coat Lacquer Finish)
- Body: Comfort Contoured Alder Body
- Neck: 1-Piece Maple, Slim Profile "D" Shape, (Fender® Flash Coat Lacquer Finish)
- Fingerboard: Slab Maple, 7.25" Radius (18.41 cm)

- Frets: 21 Vintage Style Frets
- Scale Length: 25.5" (648 mm)
- Nut: 1.650" (42 mm)
- Hardware: Nickel/Chrome
- Machine Heads: New Single Line Fender® Deluxe Vintage Tuning Machines
- Bridge: New American Vintage Synchronized Tremolo with Period-Accurate Bridge Saddles
- Pickguard: 1-Ply White (8-Hole)
- Pickups: 3 American Vintage '59 Strat® Single-Coil Pickups with Vintage White Covers
- Pickup Switching: 5-Position Blade *(original Strat guitars of this era just had a 3-Position switch)*
    - Position 1. Bridge Pickup
    - Position 2. Bridge and Middle Pickup
    - Position 3. Middle Pickup
    - Position 4. Middle and Neck Pickup
    - Position 5. Neck Pickup
- Controls: Master Volume,
    - Tone 1. (Neck Pickup),
    - Tone 2. (Middle and Bridge Pickups)
- Strings: Fender USA 250R, Nickel-Plated Steel, Gauges: (.010, .013, .017, .026, .036, .046)
- Case: Deluxe Vintage Brown Hardshell Case, P/N 0094759000
- Unique Features: Fender® Flash Coat Lacquer Finish Recreates the Finish Look and Texture from the '60s,
- Slim Profile "D" Shape Maple Neck, Comfortably Rolled Neck Edges,
- All-New Pickups Wound to Period-Correct Specs and Sound, Vintage-Accurate Bridge Saddles, Vintage-Accurate Tuner Alignment, New Aged White Knobs, Pickup Covers and Tips Bone Nut, Black Face and Side Dot Position Inlays, Butterfly String Tree, Vintage Style Heel Truss Rod Adjustment

Figure 2-13: Promo of Ritchie with Fender Stratocaster, late 1958 (©Hi-Tone Five Corp. / C3 Entertainment, used by permission)

Figure 2-14: Ritchie reaching for the high notes on his Fender Stratocaster at
The Winter Dance Party, 1959 (© Hi-Tone Five Corp. / C3 Entertainment, used by permission)

Figure 2-15: Ritchie playing his Strat. Winter Dance Party tour stop,
Kenosha, Wisconsin January 24th, 1959.
(© Hi-Tone Five Corp. / C3 Entertainment, used by permission)

Figure 2-16: Donna with Ritchie's guitar—the Gibson ES-225 and the Fender Stratocaster
with a Fender Deluxe amplifier (unknown year—possibly 1958 Narrow Panel Deluxe) on the floor.
Date unknown. (© Hi-Tone Five Corp. / C3 Entertainment, used by permission)
Source unknown—likely Valley News and Green Sheet, circa 1959–1960

Part 2: Other Instruments Associated with Ritchie

1. 1956–1958 Danelectro Longhorn 6-string Bass Guitar

This instrument should rightly be mentioned in any discussion of Ritchie's recorded music. Not so much because he played it (which he did not) on his records; but that its sound and timbre *(pronounced "tam-ber," means tonal color)* contributed so much to the overall vibe of Ritchie's sound. This is the late '50s, Danelectro Longhorn, 6-string bass guitar. It was played on Ritchie's recordings by studio guitar great, René Hall. Hall came to the 1950's and 1960's Los Angeles scene from New Orleans, where with his friend, drummer Earl Palmer, he had developed a great reputation for jazz guitar playing. Hall would play guitar on and be arranger for many sessions by several other artists, most notably Sam Cooke.

The "Dano" bass is a 6-string instrument like a standard guitar, but tuned down one octave. René Hall's use of the Dano bass was highly influential, and soon Carol Kaye, Glen Campbell, a lot of the other L.A. session greats had to carry a Dano in their arsenal to recreate that unique sound.

Figure 2-17: René Hall with Danelectro Longhorn bass that he used on some of Ritchie's recordings (date unknown, circa late 1970s–early 1980s). (Courtesy Beverly Mendheim collection, used by permission)

25

Danelectro Longhorn 6-String Bass:

- Model Number: 4623
- Year: 1958-1966
- Body: Solid-center Masonite, over pine frame
- Bridge/Tailpiece: 4-way adjustable w/Brazilian Rosewood Saddle
- Pickups: (2) Lipstick tube
- Controls: Rear-mounted, concentric volume/ tone, dual-stacked
- Pickguard: Clear plastic
  - o Early version: Apostrophe-shaped with pickups closer together
  - o Later version: Half-heart-shaped with pickups farther apart

Danelectro UB-2 6-String Bass:

- Model Number: UB-2
- Year: 1956-1958
- Body: Single-cutaway "Solid-Center" top and back Masonite, over Pine frame
- Bridge/Tailpiece:
  - o 1955: 4-way adjustable w/Brazilian Rosewood Saddle
  - o 1956 transition: chrome-plated brass bride
- Pickups: (variable 1-3) Lipstick tube
- Controls: Rear-mounted, concentric
- Pickguard: Clear plastic, with perimeter stripe and "D" logo

Figure 1-17 and 1-18: Danelectro Longhorn 6-String Bass and UB2 images and specs
(courtesy of Doug Tulloch, author, Neptune Bound: The Ultimate Danelectro Guitar Guide, used by permission)

2. Gretsch 6120 Guitar

This is the guitar that Ritchie plays on "Ooh, My Head" during the sequence of *Go Johnny Go!* It was like one of Eddie Cochran's guitars. Eddie and Ritchie were great friends. It is not Ritchie's personal guitar though; it was a rental for the movie. *(Pat Woertink correspondence, 2016–2017)*

3. Fender Amplifiers: Late 1950s-era Champ, Deluxe and Bassman Models

The electric guitar would only be a quiet piece of wood with strings that barely made any sound without an amplifier to make its voice sing above the noise of the crowd. Electric guitar amplifiers should justifiably be considered musical instruments in and of themselves. And the great guitarists "play" their amp, every bit as much as they play their guitar. Leo Fender and his crew at Fender made guitar amplifiers that were meant to be paired with their more-famous guitars as a team. Fender amps were renowned for their sonic clarity, tone, and rugged reliability. To this day, the fact that millions of guitarists still play Fender amps, speaks of Leo's skill and ingenuity those many years ago, as well as his willingness to listen to the needs of the working musician.

Leo Fender and his company were based out of Southern California, and Leo was well-known among musicians in the area. He worked originally with many of the western swing bands (country music in the Southwest was the first to popularize Fender instruments) and branched out slowly to include pop/rock acts in the area, most notably Dick Dale. Dale was a "tester" of sorts for the new gear Leo's company offered—Dale would try out amp and guitar designs of Fender's at his live gigs, and his heavy, percussive-yet-melodic guitar style would push the equipment to its limits. Dale would work with Fender to create the Dual Showman amplifiers and with JBL and Fender to create speakers would handle 100 watts of power. And Dick Dale mentored Ritchie Valens...so it would not be a stretch at all for Ritchie to play Fender guitars and amplifiers.

Not much is known about the amps that Ritchie used or owned—no paper trail of ownership or rental exists that I could find and there are very few pictures with Ritchie and an amp onstage. The few pictures that do exist show Ritchie with some flavor of Fender amp, either a Champ in his early days, or a Fender Bassman 4X10" amp at the *Live at Pacoima Jr. High* album or on the Winter Dance Party performances. The tweed (covering) Fender Deluxe and Bassman amps from this era are highly prized for their tone. The Fender Bassman 4X10" (four 10" speakers) is very celebrated by guitarists. The Bassman amp was originally designed to be a portable amp for bass players, but proved to be a bit under-powered to serve the needs of the bass player. Guitarists started plugging into the Bassman and found that they loved it.

Figure 2-20: Ritchie playing and singing "Donna" on his 1958–1959 Fender Stratocaster and two Fender Bassman 4X10" amplifiers behind him (unknown device or footswitch on top of left amp). L–R behind Ritchie: Waylon Jennings with mid-1950s Fender Precision Bass, and Tommy Allsup with late 1950s Fender Stratocaster. At the Winter Dance Party, Devine's Million Dollar Ballroom, Milwaukee, Wisconsin, January 23rd, 1959. (Photo Credit: Donna Doffing, Madison, Wisconsin / Tommy Wilde, The Rave-Eagles Club, used by permission)

In various photographs of his live gigs, Ritchie is pictured with any one of several different Fender amps; usually either a small Champ or Pro, medium-sized Deluxe, or larger Bassman. All the amps have long since gone missing out of the Valens' family collection, only the photographs survive. As such, none of the serial numbers, catalog information, or identifying markers of Ritchie's amps are known. But their dates and specifications can be approximated using period information from Fender. The following would be very similar if not identical to amps that Ritchie would have likely played through at the time.

(Specifications, ©1959 Fender Musical Instruments Corporation. Used with permission. All rights reserved.)
(Specifications from Steve Snyder, Mojotone.com, used by permission)

Fender Late 1940s or Early 1950s TV-Front Pro Guitar Amplifier Specifications

- Model/Circuit Number: 5A5, 5B5, 5C5
- Years of Production: 1947-1953
- Era: TV Front
- Configuration: Combo
- Controls: Chrome top facing w/ white screened labels, controls numbered 1-12
- Knobs: Black Chicken Head
- Faceplate
    - Front: Fuse (2A), Power Sw, Pilot Lamp, Vol, Mic Vol, Tone/Power Sw, In, In, Mic In, Mic In
    - Rear: *[unlisted]*
- Cabinet
    - Dimensions: 19 7/8" X 22" X 10" tapers to 8 3/4"
    - Hardware: Flat Leather Handle
    - Handle: Flat Leather Handle
    - Feet: Nail in Feet
    - Corners: None
- Covering Material
    - Tolex/Tweed: Vertical tweed (47-48) or diagonal tweed
    - Grill Cloth: brown mohair (47-48) or Brown linen
- Logo: Cabinet mounted, block letter
  Weight: *[unlisted]*
  Speaker
    - Size: 1 x 15"
    - Impedance: 8 ohms
    - Model: Jensen F15N (Field Coil) or Jensen P15N
- Effects: None
- Watts: 18-25 Watts
- Tubes
    - Pre-amp: Mic: 6SC7 or 12AY7 (later models) Instrument: 6SC7 or 12AY7 (later models), Phase Inverter – 6SC7 or 12AX7(later models) (paraphrase)
    - Power: 2 x metal envelope 6L6
- Bias: Cathode Biased
- Rectifier: 5U4

Fender Late 1940s or Early 1950s TV-Front Pro Guitar Amplifier—Different Circuit/ Components Specifications

- Model/Circuit Number: 5A3, 5B3
- Years of Production: 1948 – 1953
- Era: TV Front
- Configuration: Combo
- Controls: Chrome top facing w/ white screened labels, controls numbered 1-12
- Knobs: Black Chicken Head
- Faceplate
  - o Front: Pilot Lamp, Fuse (2A), Vol, Mic Vol, Tone/Power Sw, In, In, Mic In
  - o Rear: *[unlisted]*
- Cabinet
  - o Dimensions: 16 1/4 x 18 x 7 1/2
  - o Hardware: *[unlisted]*
  - o Handle: Leather
  - o Feet: Glides
  - o Corners: *[unlisted]*
- Covering Material
  - o Tolex/Tweed: Vertical Tweed (Early 48) or Diagonal Tweed
  - o Grill Cloth: Brown hohair (early 48) or linen
- Logo: Cabinet mounted, block letter
- Weight: 26 lbs
- Speaker
  - o Size: 1 x 12"
  - o Impedance: 8 ohms
  - o Model: Jensen P12R(For more info, check out the Jensen Replacement Speakers)
- Effects: *[unlisted]*
- Watts: 10-14 watts
- Tubes
  - o Pre amp: 6SN7 ; 6SC7
  - o Power: 2 x Metal Envelope 6V6
- Bias: Cathode Bias
- Rectifier: Metal Envelope 5Y3

Fender 1955 Champ Guitar Amplifier Specifications (probably SE1 or SF1 Circuit):

- Model/Circuit Number: 5E1 (55-56) 5F1 (56-64)
- Years of Production: 1955 – 1964
- Era: Narrow Panel
- Configuration: Combo
- Controls: Chrome Panel top facing w/ white screened labels, controls numbered 1-12
- Knobs: Black Chicken Head
- Faceplate:
  - o Front: In, In Vol/Power Pilot Lamp, Fuse (2A)
  - o Rear: *[unlisted]*

- Cabinet: Reproduction Tweed Champ Combo Cabinet
  - Dimensions: 11" x 12" x 7 1/4" – 5E1, 12 1/2" x 13 1/2" x 8" – 5F1
  - Hardware: [unlisted]
  - Handle: Brown Leather Handle or Black Plastic Strap ~ 1964
  - Feet: Nail-in or Chrome Glides
  - Corners: None
- Tolex/Tweed:
  - Diagonal Tweed
  - Black Tolex ~ 1964
- Grill Cloth:
  - Fender Style Oxblood w/ Gold Stripe
  - Black White Silver ~ 1964
- Logo: Cabinet Mounted, Script Fender Fullerton, California on rectangular tag
  Weight: [unlisted]
  Speaker:
  - Size: 1 x 6" or 1 x 8"
  - Impedance: 4 ohms
  - Model: Jensen p8T, Oxford 8EV or CTS AlNiCo
- Watts: 5 watts
  Tubes:
  - Pre amp: 12AX7
  - Power: 6V6GT
  - Bias: Cathode
  - Rectifier: 5Y3GT

Fender Late 1950s Deluxe Guitar Amplifier Specifications:

- Model/Circuit Number: 5E3
- Years of Production: 1955–1960
- Era: Narrow Panel
- Controls: Chrome top facing w/ white screened labels, controls numbered 1–12
- Knobs: Black Chicken Head
- Faceplate
  - Front: Ground Sw, Fuse (2A), Power Sw, Pilot Lamp, Vol, Mic Vol, Tone, In, In, Mic In, Mic In
  - Rear: [unlisted]
- Cabinet: [unlisted]
- Dimensions: 16" x 20" x 9 1/2"
- Hardware: [unlisted]
- Handle: Raised Brown Leather
- Feet: Glides
- Speaker
  - Size: 1 x 12
  - Impedance: 8 ohms
  - Model: Jensen P12R or Jensen P12Q
- Watts: 15 watts

- Tubes
    - Pre amp: 12AY7
    - Power: 2 x 6V6GT
    - Bias: Cathode Bias
    - Rectifier: 5Y3GT

Fender Late 1950s Tweed Bassman (most likely 5F6-A circuit) Guitar Amplifier Specifications:

- Model/Circuit Number: 5D6 ~ 1955, 5E6 ~ 1955, 5E6-A ~ 1955-1957, 5F6 ~ 1957, 5F6-A ~ 1958-1960
- Years of Production: 1955–1960
- Era: *[unlisted]*
- Configuration: Combo
- Controls: Chrome top facing w/ white screened labels, controls numbered 1–12
- Knobs: Black Pointer
- Faceplate: *[unlisted]*
    - Front: 5D6, 6E6: Ground Sw, Fuse (3A), Power Sw, Standby Sw, Pilot Lamp, Presense, Bass, Treb, Vol, Vol, Normal In, Bright In
    - Rear: None
- Cabinet: Reproduction Tweed Bassman Combo Cabinet
    - Dimensions: 23" x 22 1/2" x 10 1/2"
    - Hardware:
    - Handle: Raised Leather Handle, 1955–1959 or Brown Plastic Handle
    - Feet: Chrome Glides
    - Corners: None
- Tolex/Tweed:
    - Diagonal Tweed
- Grill Cloth:
    - Oxblood with Gold Stripe
- Logo: Cabinet mounted, Script
  Weight: 47 lbs
  Speaker: *[unlisted]*
- Size: 4 x 10
    - Impedance: 2 ohms
    - Model: Jensen P10R or Jensen P10Q (For more info, check out the Jensen Replacement Speakers)
- Effects: *[unlisted]*
  Watts: 40-50 watts
  Tubes
    - Pre amp: 5D6, 5E62: 2 x 12AY7
    - Power: 6D6, 5E6: 2 x 6L6G
    - Bias: Fixed; Nonadjustable
    - Rectifier: 5D6, 5E6: 2 x 5U4GA
- Comments:

  The 5F6 and 5F6-A had four speaker jacks wired in parallel under the chassis. A selenium rectifier was used in the bias circuit.

Part 3: Cassell's Music, San Fernando, California

For many decades, Cassell's Music in San Fernando, California has been the music store of choice for the region's musicians. It has a long and storied history. It is here that Ritchie, Gil and their friends rented and borrowed instruments and related gear for their gigging needs. Ed Intagliata, current manager of Cassell's, was kind to provide me a scan of the original receipt that Ritchie's mother signed in October 1958 for the Gibson ES225 guitar that is covered in the previous section. Here is a brief excerpt Ed sent me about the store, showing his continuing love for music education and the pivotal role his store has played in the community for the past 60 plus years.

"Ed Intagliata recently started his 40th year as the Owner and Manager of Cassell's Music: a store with a heart as big as can be, and one that fosters community and camaraderie among local music makers.

It was a caring spirit that first brought the Intagliata family to Cassell's Music. Intagliata's father, Salvatore, was looking for a family-run business to buy in order to fund his children's college education. In 1977, he came across Albert Cassell, who had opened his business in 1947 and who, by then, was ready to retire. After a few months of negotiations, the Intagliata family took control of Cassell's Music on January 3, 1978. Ed Intagliata, having recently graduated with a bachelor's degree in music education from Cal State Fullerton, was tasked with running his family's newly acquired music store.

'I'm the second oldest of eight siblings and, with six more children to put through college, my dad asked if I'd be willing to run a family business that would employ my five younger brothers and sisters while they were college students,' Intagliata explained. 'Without hesitation, I agreed. I worked my way through college as a part-time employee with Sears. At the time, I was mired in the customer service department…aka the complaint department. So, anything was a step up from that!'

'My expertise in music and his expertise in business were a match made in heaven,' Intagliata said, 'and we've managed to stay in business and be profitable all these years, while other stores have packed it in.' He noted that there were five or six other music stores, plus one large Guitar Center, in the area at the time that they bought the business. Only the Guitar Center remains today. All of this is a testament to Intagliata and his father's strong business acumen; their store has survived, even as the local competition has been forced to call it a day.

The family moved Cassell's Music from its original location in a downtown outdoor mall to a standalone building that they purchased on Memorial Day in 1984. The move cut the store in half: It went from 5,000 square feet to 2,500 square feet. So, Intagliata had to figure out how to maximize his space. However, he said, 'We've owned the building free and clear now for 13 years, and I sleep better at night knowing there won't be any landlord problems in the future.'

Because Cassell's Music is no longer part of a commercial strip, 'We don't have many passersbys who just wander in,' Intagliata explained. 'Whenever someone walks through our door, it was because they made a special trip to drive here. So, I like to think of our customers as friends, rather than as just customers. I want to be sure everyone is greeted promptly; they have any questions answered; and, most of all, they feel welcomed by Cassell's Music.' He continued, 'To do that means having a pleasant and friendly attitude at all times, regardless of which side of the bed you got up on.'

Over the years, Cassell's Music's customers have included some very famous faces. Seals and Crofts were frequent customers while utilizing a nearby recording studio in the 1970s, and Ritchie Valens bought his guitars at Cassell's Music. 'I have a copy of the receipt for one of them, dated October 1958, for a Gibson ES225T that his mom bought for him on payments, because he was only 17 and too young to sign the contract,' Intagliata recalled.

With Intagliata eyeing retirement in the coming years, he hopes to use his remaining working years to continue to pass on his love of music to any and all who walk through his doors.

'My life has been enriched greatly due to my involvement in music, and I desire to share that enrichment with others so that they may experience it also," Intagliata stated. 'Studies have shown that participating in music-making does so much good for an individual, and it makes them better-rounded socially. I want my love for music and music-making to be apparent to all who come into my store.'"

(© Ed Intagliata — Cassell's Music, San Fernando, CA, 2017)

Part 4: The Ritchie Valens Guitar Sound

If you want to get close to the Ritchie Valens' guitar sound for your playing and enjoyment, there are a few things to consider: First, even if you choose the right guitar and amp, and get the strings and picks Ritchie used, you will not sound truly like Ritchie. A guitarist's sound and tone are unique to them—as unique as a fingerprint. Secondly, the recording process was very different in the late 1950s, as compared to today. Analog tape recording was the norm, and studios had only two tracks or, at most, four with which to work (8-track machines were available by the late 1950s but were still rare). So, in those days, nearly all recording with a band and vocals was done live in the room. Without getting into a seminar on recording, suffice to say the combination of analog tape recording, vintage microphones, and older acoustical treatments in the rooms, made for sonic environments that were different than today's modern facilities.

Here is a list of guitars, guitar-related items and techniques to consider. It's recommended that you also spend a lot of time listening to Ritchie's recordings to get the nuances of his style:

1. A guitar with vintage single-coil pickups in it:
    a. Ritchie's H44 Harmony Stratotone had one (1) single-coil pickup
    b. Ritchie's Gibson ES-225 had two (2) P-90 single-coil pickups
    c. Ritchie's Fender Stratocaster had three (3) single-coil pickups
2. A mid-to-late 1950s Fender low-wattage tweed amplifier like a Champ, Pro, Deluxe or Bassman
    a. The lower-wattage Fender amps of the 1950s tended to "warm-up" when the volume was turned up a bit; not just get louder. These amps also had a tube rectifier that allowed for a bit more "sag" and "warmth" in the tone.
3. A capo for ease of fingerings and use of open strings
4. A very rhythmic, heavy pick attack (a combined influence of Bo Diddley, Eddie Cochran, and Dick Dale)
5. Guitar amp or studio tremolo effect—either Fender or DeArmond unit or similar (in song examples: "In a Turkish Town," "Ritchie's Blues")

CHAPTER 3
Ritchie's Music: Song Notes and Transcriptions

This chapter features brand-new, note-for-note transcriptions with guitar solos for Ritchie's best-known song "La Bamba." I have done my best to be faithful to the original recorded versions and to Ritchie's music, while bringing that music into the contemporary world just a bit. It is my sincere hope that you find these transcriptions informative, and, most of all, enjoyable to play.

Musical Notation

Ritchie did not have formal music training and couldn't read or write musical notation. However, Bob Keane was a professional clarinetist who knew the fundamentals of music very well. So, he helped Ritchie structure his ideas into recognizable song forms.

Furthermore, rock, with its two feeder genres of blues and country, was not commonly shared or otherwise communicated as a written musical form. This was especially true in its formative days of the 1950s. These are musical styles that are passed down orally/aurally from generation to generation. We do our best to blend the two approaches; understanding that it is difficult to notate the nuances of a performer like Ritchie on the written page with formal musical notation. I've written cues and phrases in places to help bridge the gap between the two.

- For the lead sheet, an octave treble clef (or the vocal tenor clef) is indicated: because Ritchie had a vocal tenor range—so the written range of the melody won't get too far from the middle of the staff. It also helps with the guitar notation.

- For the guitar solo sections, a standard treble clef is indicated: Guitar is a transposing instrument, it sounds down an octave. Guitarists still read the standard treble clef, but when they perform, the resulting sound is down an octave from concert pitch.

Part 1—Audio Tracks: "La Bamba"

In the audio portion of this book, you will hear "La Bamba" with some discussion and performance tracks. For the guitar parts, I am playing Fender Stratocaster with DiMarzio pickups, directly into a Fender Blues Deville reissue 4X10" amp.

- **Track 1**: "La Bamba": Intro riff and discussion with Ryan
- **Track 2**: "La Bamba": Full song with band *with guitar solo in the style of Ritchie Valens*
- **Track 3**: "La Bamba": Reprise of solo/verse/chorus/end—*with guitar solo in the style of Los Lobos*

Musicians:

Ryan Sheeler—lead and rhythm guitar *(center/right)*
with...
Tom Box—lead and harmony vocals, rhythm guitar (left), bass guitar
Jim Noxon—drums and percussion (claves and shaker)

Recorded at The ARK—Alexander Recording Kompany, Ames Iowa
Engineered, Mixed and Mastered by Dennis Haislip

Part 2—Song Notes: "La Bamba"

Ritchie Valens is Ritchie's one and only full-length album, composed of master tracks done at Gold Star Studios. It was released in March 1959; one month after the tragic plane crash.

"La Bamba" is the song for which Ritchie is most known. Indeed, it is one of the first and probably the best known "Latin Rock" song. The song is a traditional Mexican *huapango*—a folk song used commonly for wedding dances in the eastern Mexican region, Veracruz—and in the regional folk style known as the *son jarocho* style. Ritchie was familiar with it through his family members. It is a fusion of indigenous Mexican (Huastecan), Spanish, and African elements, and has improvisational and often-humorous element to its lyrics. An example being the repeated line "*Yo no soy marinero, soy capitán,*" meaning "I am not a sailor, I am a captain."

Figure 3-1: Ritchie Valens *album cover 1959 Del-Fi Release (©Hi-Tone Five Corp. / C3 Entertainment, used by permission)*

Ritchie learned the song from his family members; most accounts crediting his cousin Dickie Cota. Since "La Bamba" was not originally a pop song, and Ritchie was a self-taught musician, he learned to play "La Bamba" in a fluctuating meter that reflected the oral tradition, and not in straight 4/4 time of pop and rock tunes. Bob Keane first heard Ritchie playing around with the song during a car ride and convinced Ritchie to consider recording it. Initially, Ritchie didn't want to do it, because, as he felt, he didn't want to go against his heritage. But Bob convinced him. Ritchie's Aunt Ernestine helped him with the words, since he was not a native Spanish speaker. They soon worked up an arrangement with René Hall and Earl Palmer, and cut the song at Gold Star. "Donna"/"La Bamba" was a rare double-sided smash hit in February of 1959.

The intro and guitar solo to "La Bamba" are among Ritchie's best guitar work. The guitar intro is among the most famous in all of rock history—inspiring legions of songs and bands afterward. The intro is straightforward melodically—it is C, F, and G7 arpeggios strung together with a bass line walk-up and down. The intro is also a perfect example of Ritchie's lead mixed with René Hall's Danelectro six-string bass doubling the key parts of the riff.

NOTE: The entire intro riff itself is a combination of single-note picking and strumming with a slightly-improvised feel, hence some extra double-stops are written in, in places. Use the implied chords (C, F, G) to add the extra color-notes to the riff.

The guitar solo is basically entirely in the C major scale (C – D – E – F – G – A – B). However, what makes the intro and solo so great is the technique, and the attitude and forcefulness with which Ritchie plays them. The solo features a lot of quick scalar passages, rapid iterations between notes. and tremolo picking. Plus, a lot of 16th-note passages that teeter slightly off-meter, adding to the energy and drive of the solo

La Bamba

From the album Ritchie Valens *(1959)*

Traditional Arrangement by Ritchie Valens
Transcribed by Ryan Sheeler

La Bamba

From the album Ritchie Valens *(1959)*

Traditional Arrangement by Ritchie Valens
Transcribed by Ryan Sheeler

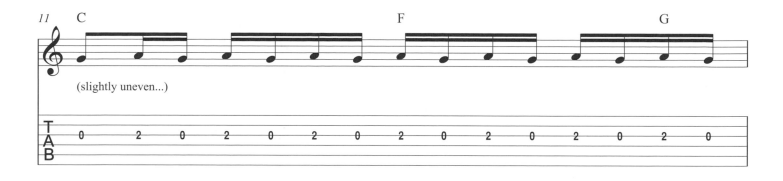

(slightly uneven...)

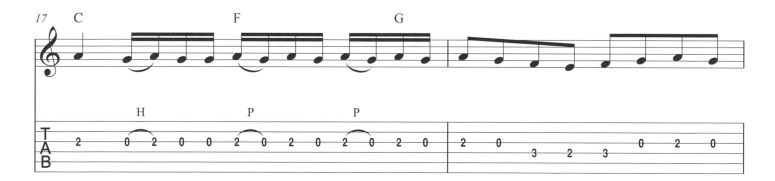

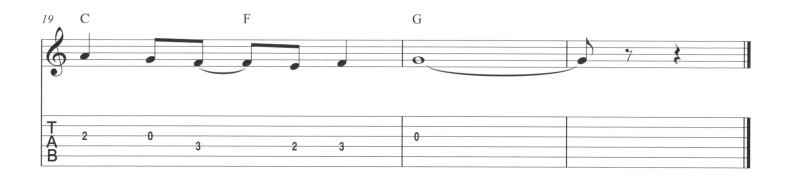

Transcription of "La Bamba": Los Lobos' Version

As an added bonus, I have included a transcription of the guitar solo in the Los Lobos' version. Guitarist Cesar Rosas performs the solo in Los Lobos' version of "La Bamba" as featured on the soundtrack to the 1987 film, *La Bamba*. Rosas' solo features a few similarities to Ritchie's original, such as melodic material based on the C major scale and tremolo picking. However, Rosas gives the solo a bit more of an updated sound and feel with his use of articulation, and with his extension of the scale down to the lower strings and up to the higher strings, in a way that Ritchie did not really do. For added flair, Rosas also makes use of "flashier" hammer-on and pull-off techniques combined with tremolo picking. The resulting solo is one that pays homage respectively to the original very well, and yet brings the sound and technique into the modern era.

La Bamba

Guitar Solo from Los Lobos' version
1987 soundtrack to the motion picture **La Bamba**

Traditional Arrangement by Ritchie Valens
Guitar Solo Arrangement (this version) by Los Lobos
Transcribed by Ryan Sheeler

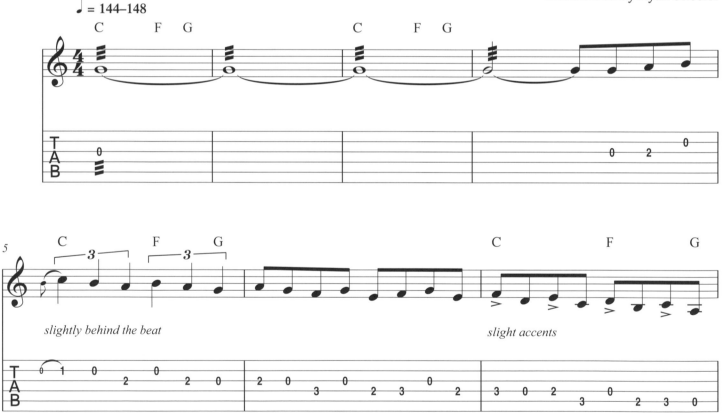

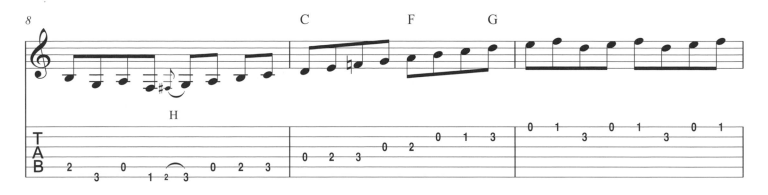

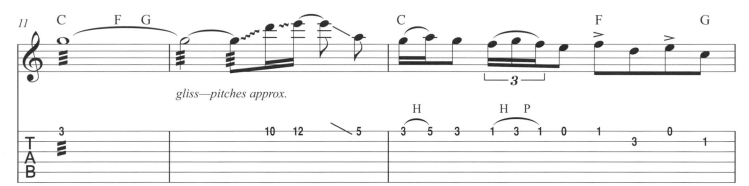

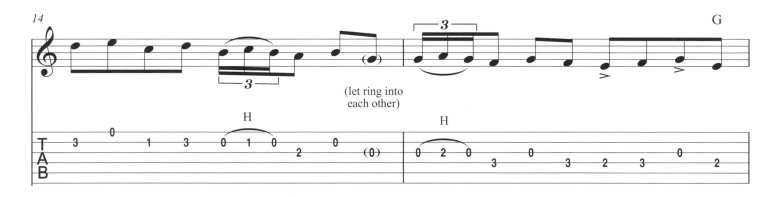

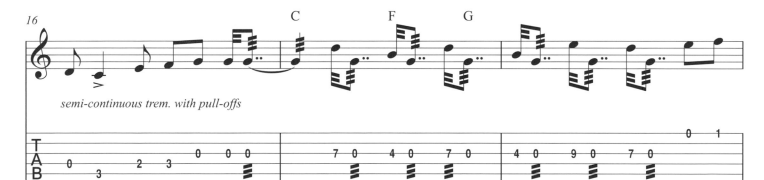

Epilogue

When Ritchie Valens died in 1959 along with Buddy Holly, J.P. Richardson and Roger Peterson, rock music suffered the first tragedy of the "Golden Age of Rock 'n' Roll." It was a major event at the time, and its magnitude has only grown in subsequent decades. While Buddy Holly was the most established star on the tour, Ritchie Valens was the hottest and fastest-rising. Ritchie's entire career was barely eight months long, and he was only 17 when he died. His entire studio recorded output barely filled two albums, but that music went on to inspire many the world over.

Unquestionably, the 1987 film *La Bamba* did a lot to both keep Ritchie in the spotlight and bring new fans to his sound. Los Lobos' versions of Ritchie's songs did an admirable job of being faithful to his sound, while bringing it into the present for a whole new generation of fans.

As I mentioned in the Introduction, I am one of those fans. For I am of the next generation that came after that era. It was my parents who turned me on to their music, which included Ritchie and many others. As I was taking my first guitar lessons, those songs left a lasting impression on my young ears, being a shy and creatively-minded child trying to find my way. And I think that was what Ritchie was doing. He had the talent, and just so happened to be in the right place at the right time. Ritchie's story is the rags-to-riches American Dream, but to stop there seems somehow unfair. Of all the great guitarists of early rock—Chuck Berry, Bo Diddley, Carl Perkins, Scotty Moore, Cliff Gallup, Eddie Cochran, Buddy Holly, Tommy Allsup, Duane Eddy, Link Wray and others—Ritchie typically isn't mentioned. By all accounts, however, many who came to know Ritchie spoke to how good of a guitarist he really was.

My hope is that this book shares some of that about Ritchie—the kind of a guitarist he was and how much he loved the instrument. His music features a lot of great riffs, solos, and phrases. As mentioned previously, some of these were played by René Hall, but Ritchie did perform nearly all his own solos and riffs. Throughout this book, I've tried to capture some of the facets of Ritchie's style and bring them to bear on Ritchie's legacy. I hope you've enjoyed this journey with me down musical memory lane, as we pay tribute to one of the founders of Chicano rock 'n' roll—one of the all-time greats, *Ritchie Valens*.

Ryan Bleeler

Acknowledgments

First, I need to thank my Lord and Savior, Jesus Christ. Many times, I felt your guiding hand over this project and I am thankful for your presence in my life.

This project would not have been possible if not for the help and guidance of the following. I am so grateful for your help, your knowledge, and your willingness to share your love of Ritchie and his music.

- The Valens Family—Connie Valens and The Valens Family / *Hi-Tone Five, Corp*—I am deeply grateful for all you have done to keep Ritchie's music and legacy alive. I've very thankful for the time, advice, leads, and information you've given me. I hope this book is a worthy addition to Ritchie's legacy

- Ani Khachoian and Peter Bertucci / *C3 Entertainment*—Thank you so much for your assistance of the licensing and images.

- Ron Middlebrook / *Centerstream* Publishing—thank you for believing in my project

- Charylu Roberts and Ronny Schiff / *O.Ruby Publications*—thank you for believing in my project

- Tom Box and Jim Noxon (my fellow band mates from The Box Brothers Band, Ames IA) – thanks for lending your talents to the recording.

- Dennis Haislip / *Alexander Recording Kompany, Ames IA*—thanks for your studio talents and great listening to make these recordings the best they can be.

- Pat Woertink / *Legend Gold Records*—thanks so much for your great insights on Ritchie's gear and his music, guitars and rock 'n' roll in general. Your love of Ritchie's music, and your long association with Ritchie's family have been great fun to learn about.

- Beverly Mendheim—you have really been a tremendous help. Thank you for all your advice, research help, and great conversations about all things music.

- Sal Gutierrez / *Norman's Rare Guitars*—Thank you so much for your great insights into Ritchie's music and your keen eye for guitars and music.

- Gil Rocha—along with the Valens Family, you have such wonderful first-hand memories of Ritchie and his musical development. Thanks so much for all your help and insight.

- Carol Kaye—thank you so much for your wonderful musicianship, insight and contributions to the music of Los Angeles in rock, pop, jazz and film for the last fifty-plus years. I have tremendous respect for all you have done. And, I am incredibly thankful for the pieces of information you've provided not just to me, but to many faithful students of music, and of those times.

- Gail Smith—thank you for the use of the photos and your unique role in helping to keep Ritchie's legacy alive.

- Crystal Jackson, *Pacoima Stories/Crystal Jackson Productions*—your passion for Pacoima and its history is so contagious, I was immediately drawn into the story of this fascinating town and the role it played in Ritchie's music and upbringing.

- Jose Padilla—Pacoima, California

- Joe Vinikow—Archtop.com; www.archtop.com

- Doug Tulloch, author of "Neptune Bound: The Ultimate Danelectro Guitar Guide"

- Ed Intagliata—*Cassell's Music*, San Fernando, CA

- Diane Taylor—*Trader's Loan and Jewelry,* Reseda, CA

- Mojotone / Ampwares—Steve Snyder

- Harmony Guitars Database—Jan Demont

- Donna Doffing—Madison, Wisconsin

- Tommy Wilde—*Eagles Club/The Rave*, Milwaukee, Wisconsin

- Jim McCool and Sevan Garabedian—Blue Days Productions, Madison, Wisconsin

- Sheryl and Sherry Davis—*The Surf Speaks*

- The Surf Ballroom—Clear Lake, IA, and everyone in the extended "February Family"—it is so much fun to join you every year for the Winter Dance Party and share the music and memories.

Bibliography

I. Books

- Keane, Bob. *The Oracle of Del-Fi*. Del-Fi International Books, 2006.
- Lehmer, Larry. *The Day the Music Died*. New York: Schirmer Trade Books, 2000.
- Mendheim, Beverly. *Ritchie Valens: The First Latino Rocker*. Tempe: Arizona State University, Bilingual Review Press, 1987.
- Reyes, David and Tom Waldman. *Land of a Thousand Dances: Chicano Rock 'n' Roll from Southern California*. Albuquerque: University of New Mexico Press, 2009.
- Schermer, Tony. *Backbeat: Earl Palmer's Story*. Cambridge: Da Capo Press, 2000.
- Tulloch, Doug. *Neptune Bound: The Ultimate Danelectro Guitar Guide*. Centerstream, 2008.
- Wheeler, Tom. *The Stratocaster Chronicles: Celebrating 50 Years of the Fender Strat*. Milwaukee: Hal Leonard, 2007.
- Wheeler, Tom. *The Soul of Tone: The History of Fender Amps*. Milwaukee: Hal Leonard, 2007.

II. Compact Discs, Audio Recordings, and Liner Notes

- Valens, Ritchie. *Ritchie Valens*. Wounded Bird, 2006. (Original release Del-Fi Records, 1959).
- Valens, Ritchie. *Ritchie*. Wounded Bird, 2006. (Original release Del-Fi Records, 1959).
- Valens, Ritchie. *In Concert at Pacoima Jr. High*. Wounded Bird, 2006. CD. (Original release Del-Fi Records, 1960).
- Valens, Ritchie. *The Ritchie Valens Story*. Del-Fi, 1993.
- Valens, Ritchie. *Come On, Let's Go!* Del-Fi Records, 1998. (CD box set).
- Various Artists. *La Bamba: Original Motion Picture Soundtrack*. Rhino/Slash, 1987

III. Films and Documentaries

- *Chicano Rock!: The Sounds of East Los Angeles*. Directed by Jon Wilkman, PBS, 2009.
- *Go, Johnny, Go!* Directed by Paul Landres, Hal Roach Productions/Valiant Films, 1959.
- *La Bamba*. Directed by Luis Valdez. Produced by Taylor Hackford. Columbia Pictures, 1987.
- *Pacoima Stories*, Crystal Jackson Productions. Pacoima, California, 2016.
- *The Ritchie Valens Story/The Complete Ritchie Valens*, Whirlwind Media, Inc. 2000.

IV. Research Articles

- Alisau, Patricia. "Un poco de gracia. (Veracruz and other Mexican cities)." *Business Mexico*, June 2001, Vol.11(6), p.65.
- Avant-Mier, Roberto. "Latinos in the Garage: A Genealogical Examination of the Latino/a Presence and Influence in Garage Rock (and Rock and Pop Music)." *Popular Music and Society:* Vol. 31, No. 5: December 2008, pp. 555–574.
- Harwood, Ian. "Capo tasto (capo)" *The New Grove Dictionary of Music and Musicians*. Edited by Stanley Sadie and J. Tyrrell. London: Macmillan, 2001. Vol.5, p.96.
- Laing, Dave. "Valens, Ritchie" The New Grove Dictionary of Music and Musicians. Edited by Stanley Sadie and J. Tyrrell. London: Macmillan, 2001. Vol.26, p.205–6.
- Macias, Anthony. "Bringing Music to the People: Race, Urban Culture, and Municipal Politics in Postwar Los Angeles." *American Quarterly*, Vol. 56, No. 3, Los Angeles and the Future of Urban Cultures (Sep.2004), pp. 693–717.
- Stacy, Lee. "Valens, Ritchie." *Mexico and The United States*. New York: Marshall Cavendish. Vol 3., pp.883–5, 2003
- "Reintroducing the harmony guitar line: harmony, the world's most popular guitar brand for close to a century, is coming back with a faithful reissue of the famous Ritchie Valens model." *Music Trades* Feb. 2008: 140+. *Biography in Context*. Web. 15 Oct. 2016.

V. Correspondence

- Burns, Bob (Gibson Guitars). "Re: Ritchie Valens project addition: Gibson ES-175." Message to Ryan Sheeler. 17–21 Nov 2016. Email.
- Callier, Karen (GAC). "Ritchie Valens." Message to Ryan Sheeler. 17 April 2016. Email.
- Gutierrez, Sal. "Re: Ritchie's guitars." Message to Ryan Sheeler. 30 March 2016. Email.
- Gutierrez, Sal. "Re: Gil Rocha—guitars." Message to Ryan Sheeler. 11 April 2016. Email.
- Gutierrez, Sal. "Danelectro with Rene Hall Picture." Message to Ryan Sheeler. 28 April 2016. Email.
- Gutierrez, Sal. "Ritchie Pacoima Jr. High Close up." Message to Ryan Sheeler. 15 May 2016. Email.
- Gutierrez, Sal. "From Sal G. Re: Ritchie picture." Message to Ryan Sheeler. 15 May 2016. Email.
- Gutierrez, Sal. Phone conversation. 09 April 2016.
- Gutierrez, Sal. Phone conversation. 24 April 2016.
- Gutierrez, Sal. Phone conversation. 14 May 2016.
- Gutierrez, Sal. Phone conversation. 15 July 2017.
- Gruhn, George. "Ritchie's guitars." Message to Ryan Sheeler. 05 September 2016. Email.
- Intagliata, Ed. "Richie Valens / Cassells Music." Message to Ryan Sheeler. 31 March 2016 — 26 April 2016. Email.
- Intagliata, Ed. "Re: Ritchie picture with Fender 1958." Message to Ryan Sheeler. 09 August 2016. Email.
- Intagliata, Ed. "Re: Other music stories in Pacoima in 1950s." Message to Ryan Sheeler. 09 August 2016. Email.
- Intagliata, Ed. "Re: Ritchie—different Gibson guitar." Message to Ryan Sheeler. 18 August 2016. Email.
- Intagliata, Ed. "Re: Cassell's short bio." Message to Ryan Sheeler. 12 July 2017. Email.
- Jackson, Crystal. Phone conversation. 13 July 2016.
- Jackson, Crystal. "Re: Pacoima 1950s radio stations." Message to Ryan Sheeler. 21 July 2016. Email.
- Jackson, Crystal. "Re: Pacoima—Sears store in the 1950s." Message to Ryan Sheeler. 22 July 2016. Email.
- Jackson, Crystal. "Re: Pacoima 1950s music stories." Message to Ryan Sheeler. 08 August 2016. Email.
- Jackson, Crystal. "Ritchie Valens." Message to Ryan Sheeler. 24 August 2016. Email.
- Jackson, Crystal. "Re: Crest Loan and Jewelry, Pacoima." Message to Ryan Sheeler. 08 September 2016. Email.
- Jackson, Crystal. "Re: Rennie's Theater, Pacoima." Message to Ryan Sheeler. 03 November 2016. Email.
- Jackson, Crystal. "Re: Valley News and Green Sheet paper." 29 April 2017. Email.
- Kaye, Carol. "Re: Ritchie Valens—Guitars research project." Message to Ryan Sheeler. 13-14 February 2016. Email.
- Kaye, Carol. "Re: René Hall—Dano question and amps." Message to Ryan Sheeler. 24 February 2016. Email.
- Kaye, Carol. "Re: Danelectro with René Hall picture." Message to Ryan Sheeler. 24–29 Feb 2016. Email.
- Kaye, Carol. "Re: Ritchie—Gibson ES225." Message to Ryan Sheeler. 25 April 2016. Email.
- Kaye, Carol. "Re: Earl Palmer and Ritchie." Message to Ryan Sheeler. 07 June 2016. Email.
- Kaye, Carol. "Re: Ritchie Valens different Gibson guitar." Message to Ryan Sheeler. 15 Nov 2016. Email.
- Mendheim, Beverly. Phone conversation. 31 May 2016.
- Mendheim, Beverly. "Re: Ritchie Valens—follow up." Message to Ryan Sheeler. 02–03 June 2016. Email.
- Mendheim, Beverly. "Re: Bob Keane and Ritchie." Message to Ryan Sheeler. 07 June 2016. Email.
- Mendheim, Beverly. "Re: In a Turkish Town//Ba Bendi Bendi" (Indonesian folk song). Message to Ryan Sheeler. 07 June 2016. Email.
- Mendheim, Beverly. "Re: Pacoima or Los Angeles Radio Stations 1950s." Message to Ryan Sheeler. 22 July 2017. Email.
- Mendheim, Beverly. "Re: Ritchie — pictures in the studio." Message to Ryan Sheeler. 06 August 2017. Email.
- Mendheim, Beverly. "Re: more Ritchie—Fender guitar." Message to Ryan Sheeler. 04 September 2016. Email.
- Mendheim, Beverly. "Re: Ritchie's green Harmony Stratotone." Message to Ryan Sheeler. 11 September 2016. Email.
- Mendheim, Beverly. "Re: Ritchie transcriptions." Message to Ryan Sheeler. 10–14 October 2016. Email.
- Mendheim, Beverly. "Re: Ritchie's American Legion gig." Message to Ryan Sheeler. 20, 28–29 October 2016. Email.
- Mendheim, Beverly. "Re: Ritchie—white guitar." Message to Ryan Sheeler. 23 Nov 2016. Email.
- Mendheim, Beverly. "Re: Ritchie's Guitars." Message to Ryan Sheeler. 01–03 Jan 2017. Email.
- Mendheim, Beverly. "Re: The Lost Tapes." Message to Ryan Sheeler. 06 Jan 2017. Email.
- Mendheim, Beverly. "Re: René Hall Danelectro picture." Message to Ryan Sheeler. 09 Jan 2017.
- Rocha, Gil. Phone conversation. 28 May 2016.
- Rocha, Gil. Phone conversation. 16 July 2016.
- Rocha, Gil. Phone conversation. 21 July 2016.

- Rocha, Gil. Phone conversation. 20 August 2016.
- Rocha, Gil. Phone conversation. 30 November 2016.
- Rocha, Gil. "Re: Ritchie pictures." Message to Ryan Sheeler. 14–15 November 2016. Email.
- Rocha, Gil. "Re: Ritchie—white guitar." Message to Ryan Sheeler. 21 November 2016. Email.
- Rocha, Gil. "Re: Fwd: Re: Ritchie Valens project addition: Gibson ES-175." Message to Ryan Sheeler. 22 November 2016. Email.
- Rocha, Gil. "Re: Rennie's Theater." Message to Ryan Sheeler. 06 January 2016. Email.
- Smith, Gail. "RE: Ritchie guitar pictures." 30 July 2016. Email (Facebook messenger)
- Snyder, Steve (Mojotone.com). "Re: Fender amps—Ritchie Valens' project." 07 March–07 November 2016. Email.
- Snyder, Steve (Mojotone.com). "Re: Ritchie Valens — old Fender champ?." 07 March–07 November 2016. Email.
- Stout, Tierney (Gibson Guitars). "Re: Ritchie Valens Gibson ES225 request." Message to Ryan Sheeler. 11–17 July 2017. Email
- Tulloch, Doug. "Re: Danelectro Bass question—Ritchie Valens project" Message to Ryan Sheeler. 20–21 March 2016. Email.
- Valens, Connie. "Re: Question: Ritchie and guitar." Message to Ryan Sheeler. 24 March 2015. Email.
- Valens, Connie. "Re: Ritchie's guitars." Message to Ryan Sheeler. 02 February 2015. Email.
- Valens, Connie. "Re: Rare Ritchie pic." Message to Ryan Sheeler. 28 June 2016. Email.
- Valens, Connie. "Re: Ritchie's original green Harmony guitar." Message to Ryan Sheeler. 15–16 July 2016. Email.
- Valens, Connie. "Re: Ritchie album covers — permissions." Message to Ryan Sheeler. 22 July 2016. Email.
- Valens, Connie. "Re: Picture permissions." Message to Ryan Sheeler. 29 July 2016. Email.
- Valens, Connie. "Re: Ritchie Picture — Fender Strat 1958?" Message to Ryan Sheeler. 11–26 August 2016. Email.
- Valens, Connie. "Re: Ritchie guitar for recording — different guitar." Message to Ryan Sheeler. 15–18 August 2016. Email.
- Valens, Connie. "Re: Book Project and Fall 2017 — photo request." Message to Ryan Sheeler. 12 July 2017. Email. •
- Valens, Connie "Ritchie's Harmony Guitar." Phone conversation. 06 May 2019.
- Vinikow, Joe. "Re: Ritchie Valens — white acoustic guitar. 04, 21 March 2016. Email.
- Wells, Bryce (Fender Consumer Relations). "Re: [Fender] Re: Re: [Fender] Re: American Vintage '59 Strats — Ritchie Valens project." Message to Ryan Sheeler. 23 March 2016 —03 Aug 2016. Email.
- Wells, Bryce (Fender Consumer Relations). "Re: Ritchie Valens project — amps." Message to Ryan Sheeler. 7–25 Nov 2016. Email.
- Wells, Bryce (Fender Consumer Relations). "Re: Ritchie Valens — Fender champ?." Message to Ryan Sheeler. 22 Nov 2016. Email.
- Woertink, Pat. Phone conversation. 05 March 2016.
- Woertink, Pat. Phone conversation. 08 May 2016.
- Woertink, Pat. Phone conversation. 27 August 2016.
- Woertink, Pat. Phone conversation. 10 September 2016.
- Woertink, Pat. Phone conversation. 26 November 2016.
- Woertink, Pat "Ritchie's Harmony Guitar." Phone conversation. 06 May 2019.

VI. External Websites

- Carol Kaye—http://www.carolkaye.com

- Fender Guitars—http://www.fender.com

- Gibson Guitars—http://www.gibson.com

- G&L Guitars / BBE Sound—http://glguitars.com/

- Gold Star Recording Studios—http://www.goldstarrecordingstudios.com/

- Harmony Guitar Database—http://harmony.demont.net/

- Mojotone/Ampwares—http://www.mojotone.com | http://www.ampwares.com

- The Official Ritchie Valens Website—http://www.ritchievalens.com

- Joe Viniwork—http://www.archtop.com

About the Author...

RYAN SHEELER is a guitarist, composer and author from Iowa. He is a Lecturer in the Department of Music at Iowa State University where he teaches the History of American Rock 'n' Roll. He co-authored *From Bakersfield to Beale Street: A Regional History of American Rock 'n' Roll* with David Stuart and is also the author of *Playing for Eternity: Resource Guide for the Electric Guitarist in Worship.*

He received his M.A. in Interdisciplinary Graduate Studies (Music Composition/Musicology) from Iowa State in 2006, and his B.A. in Music from Iowa State in 1997, with additional graduate study in Music Theory/Music History at the University of Iowa School of Music.

A multi-genre artist/composer, Ryan has performed with regional rock bands such as The Box Brothers, Flying Taxi, and The Rag Doll Incident, in a variety of venues and settings. He has performed for the national Broadway tour of *Chicago*, and regional performances of *Fiddler on the Roof, Rent, Grease, Joseph and the Amazing Technicolor Dreamcoat*, and *Pippin*. Ryan composes for many ensembles—large and small—and has won awards from ASCAP and the Iowa Motion Picture Association. In addition, he has several recordings of his own music available through his website: http://www.ryansheeler.com.

His research interests are varied: American popular and roots music (especially blues, country, early rock, and gospel music of the 1930s–1960s); the 1959 Winter Dance Party tour; Christian worship arts and theology; and guitar pedagogy. He is a member of the Ames Community Arts Council, Central Iowa Blues Society, The Iowa Composers Forum, and the Iowa Rock 'n' Roll Music Association.

More Great Guitar Books from Centerstream...